Coop Invader

"The Opossum You Never Knew"

Pinkie-Pepper & Papa-Pepper

Coop Invader

Copyright © 2022

All rights reserved.

ISBN: **9798413267332**

DEDICATION

This book is dedicated to all those who enjoy reading, and to all who like learning about the amazing animals that God created.

Coop Invader

DISCLAIMER:

Please note this book features photos of humans holding wild animals. Wild animals can be unpredictable and should be left in the wild. It is not recommended that you handle them or try to catch them. Decades of experience came into play while we took the photos for this book. That said, please enjoy the story.

Coop Invader

Big Brother and Little Brother live on a homestead where they have a garden and raise animals.
It is Big Brother's job to teach Little Brother how to do chores and be responsible.

Feeding the chickens is the first chore of the morning. Big Brother opens the lid of the feed bin and they peek inside.

Although Little Brother is small, he is big enough to feed the chickens. Using a gourd that is shaped like a spoon, he scoops the feed while Big Brother watches.

The feed is poured into a pan so it does not get scattered and wasted. Now it is time to let the chickens out of the coop so they can eat their breakfast.

Eagerly, the chickens rush out into the fresh, morning air and dig in. The rooster keeps watch for danger while the hungry hens enjoy breakfast.

With the chickens now out of the coop, it is time for the brothers to collect the eggs for their breakfast.

The fresh eggs are fragile, so Little Brother must be very gentle when collecting them. Big Brother carefully watches him, but suddenly hears a sound behind them.

Startled, Big Brother turns around. Up in the corner of the coop a strange animal is lurking!

Surprised, the brothers gasp and stare. "What is it?" Little Brother wonders.

Coop Invader

It looks like a giant rat that is the size of a cat, but it has climbed up the wall like a monkey.

Coop Invader

"Run!" shouts Big Brother.
"Go get Papa!"

As quickly as he can run, Little Brother is out of the coop. Papa will know what to do, and what kind of animal it is.

Excited and afraid, Little Brother does not want to leave Big Brother alone with the creature for long, so he races to find Papa.

Soon, Papa joins the boys back at the coop. Little Brother shows him where the creature is hiding. "Are you going to kill it, Papa?" Big Brother asks.

Coop Invader

Papa thinks for a moment and says, "There is no need for that, boys." He fixes his gloves and tells his sons, "Stay back."

Cautiously, Papa climbs up the chicken roosting bars until he's high enough to reach the animal. Slowly, he reached out his hand and grabs the creatures' tail.

The animal is startled and confused, but it does not attack as Papa gently, but firmly, picks it up and brings it down.

Coop Invader

Papa turns and shows the boys. "This is an opossum," he explains. "Most people just call them 'possums, but it is spelled opossum."

"It must have been looking for a meal; maybe an egg or a little chicken. It is a good thing you boys came out to do your morning chores when you did. It probably snuck in here last night."

"What did you say it is called, Papa?"
Little Brother asks.
"An opossum," Papa answers. "Would you like to learn some neat things about opossums?"

"Yes, Sir!" the boys answer in unison. "Well, thankfully I know quite a bit about opossums," Papa says.

Coop Invader

"Have you children ever heard anyone use the expression 'playing 'possum?' It can mean pretending to be dead or faking being asleep. People use this phrase because opossums can pretend to be dead when they feel threatened."

"It is one of their defense mechanisms that protects them from predators. If an animal was going to try to kill the opossum, playing dead can trick it into thinking the opossum is already dead. When the predator loses interest the opossum stops pretending and gets back up."

Coop Invader

"When baby opossums are born they are called 'joeys,' just like baby kangaroos. This is because opossums are marsupials too, just like kangaroos, koalas, and wombats. Most marsupials live in Australia. The only one found in the United States is the opossum."

"Like other marsupials, mother opossums keep their young in a pouch. Hairless joeys are born very tiny and have to climb up into the pouch. They live in the pouch until they are a couple months old."

"Inside the pouch is where the mother opossum's teats are. Like other mammals, baby opossums drink milk from their mother. The joeys will nurse for about three months, and keep their eyes closed for most of that time."

"Baby opossum joeys are called Jacks and Jills. The boys are called Jacks and the girls are called Jills."

Coop Invader

"While opossums may look like big rats with long rat-like tails, their tails are actually prehensile, like some monkeys have. This means that they can grasp things with their tails, and even hang upside-down from trees."

"Opossums are very good at climbing. They use this skill to escape from predators. If you see an opossum, and if it does not play dead, often it will climb up a tree to get away from you."

"If an opossum doesn't play dead or run away, it may hiss at you and show off its sharp teeth. Opossums have fifty teeth, more than any other North American mammal. They will also drool, which can make them look dangerous or sick. If an opossum opens its mouth at you, you should walk away because they can bite."

Coop Invader

"On a farm or homestead, opossums will eat eggs and smaller poultry. Secure pens and coops are the best way to protect your animals from hungry opossums. Did you know they can even kill horses? It's not because they attack them though..."

Coop Invader

"The reason opossums are dangerous to horses is because they can transmit a parasite called EPM (Equine Protozoal Myeloencephalitis.) Eggs from the parasite can be shed in the opossums' feces."

"If an opossum poops on horse feed or hay, and the horse eats the infected feces, the horse can get the EPM parasite which causes neurological damage and can even lead to death. It is best to keep horse feed in a covered container."

Coop Invader

Coop Invader

"Venomous snakes can hurt or even kill a lot of different animal species. However, opossums are not affected by snake venom and they can even receive multiple bites without getting sick or dying. They are also resistant to scorpion venom and bee stings."

"One good thing that opossums do is eat ticks. Ticks like wood ticks and deer ticks are types of external parasites that like to climb on animals and suck their blood. Some even carry diseases, like Lyme's disease."

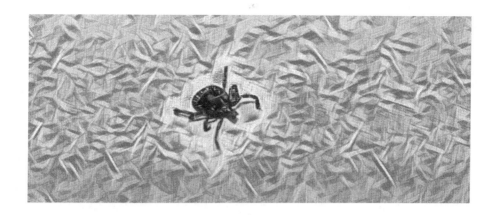

"When ticks climb on opossums, the opossums will groom themselves and eat the ticks. An opossum can eat thousands of ticks each week, which means there are less ticks that can climb on us."

Coop Invader

"While opossums can bite if they feel threatened, they almost never get rabies. Most likely it is due to their lower body temperature. This one seems pretty gentle, but it will be best if we move it off of our homestead."

Coop Invader

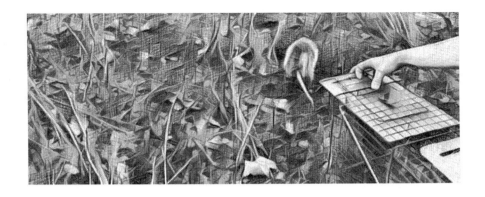

Papa puts the opossum in a cage and they head out into the woods to release it. There is no need to kill it, and opossums are probably much more beneficial than many people realize. At the woods edge Papa opens the cage and the opossum races out.

Coop Invader

The opossum doesn't waste any time playing dead or hissing. Instead it climbs up the first tree it finds, free to live another day. As it peers down at the brothers, Big Brother and Little Brother marvel at this incredible creature.

Coop Invader

The End.

Coop Invader

ABOUT THE AUTHORS

The writing of this book was a joint effort between Pinkie-Pepper and Papa-Pepper. They wanted to create a fact-filled fiction book to help educate people of all ages on the amazing creature that is the opossum. This daddy-daughter team once partnered with a third generation and brought one of Grandpa-Pepper's tales to life in the volume <u>Armadillo Escape: The Adventures of Farmer Z</u>. This book was their first venture co-writing a book together.

Coop Invader

ABOUT "LITTLE BROTHER"

"Little Brother" was played by Buddy-Pepper, AKA "Bugger." He's a happy little boy who likes climbing trees like opossums do. He is very helpful and appreciates a lot of the wild creatures he encounters on his family's homestead and in the wild while enjoying adventures and life.

Coop Invader

ABOUT "BIG BROTHER"

"Big Brother" was played by "Monster Truck the Pepper," an actual big brother who is the oldest boy of Mama & Papa-Pepper. He enjoys learning a lot about animals and even teaches his younger siblings about chores and being responsible in real life, just like in the story.

Coop Invader

ABOUT "PAPA"

"Papa" was played by Papa-Pepper, a wild-man of a homesteader and happily married father of seven. Over the years he's learned a lot about many animals including opossums, and even discovered that opossums are biofluorescent under ultra-violet lighting. He enjoys interacting with opossums and other animals that wander onto his homestead. His blog can be found on steemit.com and hive.blog, and his videos are available on the "Papa Pepper" YouTube channel.

Coop Invader

ABOUT THE OPOSSUM

The opossum was played by "Megan," a wild opossum who wandered onto the Abundant Harvest Homestead where the Little-Peppers live. She cooperated well for her scenes during the photo shoot. She enjoys munching on ticks and long walks through the woods on moonlit nights. Several other opossums were also photographed for this project.

Coop Invader

ABOUT THE PHOTOGRAPHER

Red-Pepper, Awesome the 'Possum, & Pinkie-Pepper (left to right)

Pinkie-Pepper (above right) took the photos for this project when she was ten years old. She is the oldest of seven children, and a talented young lady indeed. When she's not photographing opossums or her younger brothers, she enjoys caring for baby lambs, riding her pony, and hatching a variety of poultry at the Abundant Harvest Homestead.

Coop Invader

Check out our other books:

ARMADILLO ESCAPE
The Adventures of Farmer Z

Story by Grandpa-Pepper
Photos by Pinkie-Pepper

A three generation project and entertaining children's tale.

Coop Invader

Check out our other books:

WHY WE HOMESTEAD

By Kevin "Papa-Pepper" Ziolkowski

The personal testimony of "Papa-Pepper" on why our family chose to move out to the country and homestead.

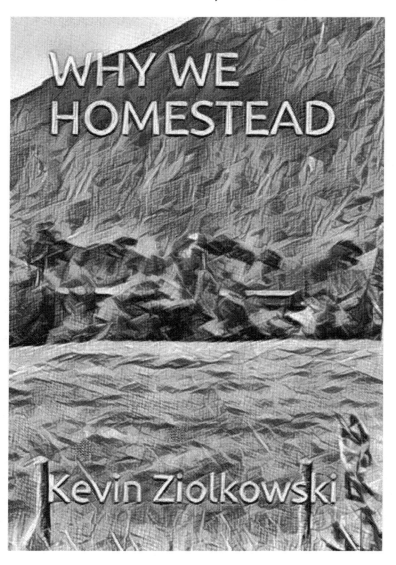

Coop Invader

Check out our other books:

50 DAYS TO UNDERSTANDING THE END-TIMES MORE ACCURATELY

By Kevin "Papa-Pepper" Ziolkowski

A look into the end-times based on what is revealed in the Bible. A solid read for anyone interested in Bible prophecy about the end of days.

Made in the USA
Middletown, DE
13 August 2022

70429286R00045